MY INFO BOOK

TITLE_____

_____

_____

SUBTITLE_____

_____

BOOK
SERIES_____

_____

BOOK#_____

PUBLISHED ON_____

Searchtower Publishers

Copyright

write
pic

CONTENTS

My Books Info

Keep track of the details of your book.

The profiles of your characters, and places. Your important foreshadowing, details of each chapter, and the little butterfly moments that can be used in the description of your book to the iiiiiiiiiii line on the cover.

20 CHARACTERS PROFILES

Check off when each detail is mentioned in your book. You may have thought you mentioned it but didn't. You could also jot down the chapter number it was mentioned in.

CHARACTER 1

FIRST_____MIDDLE_____LAST_____

NICKNAME_____

HAIR_COLOR_____STYLE_____

EYES_____GLASSES_____CONTACTS_____

SKIN_TONE_____TYPE_____

BUILD_____HEIGHT_____

D.O.B._____AGE_____

PLACE_OF_BIRTH_____

IDENTIFING_MARKS_____

CLOTHES_____

HEALTH_____

MOTHER_____

FATHER_____

SISTERS_____

BROTHERS_____

OTHER_FAMILY_____

HOME_LIFE_____

HOME_____LIVES_WITH_____

WORK_____DRIVES_____

SKILLS_____

SCHOOL_____

PETS_____

FRIENDS_____

GATHERING_PLACE_____

PHYSICAL_HABITS_____

VERBAL_HABITS_____

PEEVES_____

PERSONAL_ITEM_____

INTROVERT_____OR_EXTROVERT_____

TANGIBLE_THINGS_____OR_ABSTRACT_THINGS_____

TRUTH_&_LOGIC_____OR_ISSUES_&_CAUSES_____

STRUCTURED_____OR_UNSTRUCTURED_____

2

LIKES_____

DISLIKES_____

HOBBIES_____

TALENT_____

MEMMORY_OF_____
_____

GOALS_____
_____

FEARS_____
_____

KNOWS_____
_____
_____

DOESN'T_KNOW_____
_____
_____
_____

OTHER_____
_____
_____
_____
_____
_____
_____
_____
_____
_____
_____
_____
_____
_____
_____

CHARACTER 2

FIRST_____MIDDLE_____LAST_____

NICKNAME_____

HAIR_COLOR_____STYLE_____

EYES_____GLASSES_____CONTACTS_____

SKIN_TONE_____TYPE_____

BUILD_____HEIGHT_____

D.O.B._____AGE_____

PLACE_OF_BIRTH_____

IDENTIFING_MARKS_____

CLOTHES_____

HEALTH_____

MOTHER_____

FATHER_____

SISTERS_____

BROTHERS_____

OTHER_FAMILY_____

HOME_LIFE_____

HOME_____LIVES_WITH_____

WORK_____DRIVES_____

SKILLS_____

SCHOOL_____

PETS_____

FRIENDS_____

GATHERING_PLACE_____

PHYSICAL_HABITS_____

VERBAL_HABITS_____

PEEVES_____

PERSONAL_ITEM_____

INTROVERT_____OR_EXTROVERT_____

TANGIBLE_THINGS_____OR_ABSTRACT_THINGS_____

TRUTH_&_LOGIC_____OR_ISSUES_&_CAUSES_____

STRUCTURED_____OR_UNSTRUCTURED_____

4

LIKES_____

DISLIKES_____

HOBBIES_____

TALENT_____

MEMMORY_OF_____
_____

GOALS_____
_____

FEARS_____
_____

KNOWS_____
_____
_____

DOESN'T_KNOW_____
_____
_____
_____

OTHER_____
_____
_____
_____
_____
_____
_____
_____
_____
_____
_____
_____
_____

CHARACTER 3

FIRST_____MIDDLE_____LAST_____

NICKNAME_____

HAIR_COLOR_____STYLE_____

EYES_____GLASSES_____CONTACTS_____

SKIN_TONE_____TYPE_____

BUILD_____HEIGHT_____

D.O.B._____AGE_____

PLACE_OF_BIRTH_____

IDENTIFING_MARKS_____

CLOTHES_____

HEALTH_____

MOTHER_____

FATHER_____

SISTERS_____

BROTHERS_____

OTHER_FAMILY_____

HOME_LIFE_____

HOME_____LIVES_WITH_____

WORK_____DRIVES_____

SKILLS_____

SCHOOL_____

PETS_____

FRIENDS_____

GATHERING_PLACE_____

PHYSICAL_HABITS_____

VERBAL_HABITS_____

PEEVES_____

PERSONAL_ITEM_____

INTROVERT_____OR_EXTROVERT_____

TANGIBLE_THINGS_____OR_ABSTRACT_THINGS_____

TRUTH_&_LOGIC_____OR_ISSUES_&_CAUSES_____

STRUCTURED_____OR_UNSTRUCTURED_____

LIKES_____

DISLIKES_____

HOBBIES_____

TALENT_____

MEMMORY_OF_____

_____

GOALS_____

_____

FEARS_____

_____

KNOWS_____

_____

_____

DOESN'T_KNOW_____

_____

_____

_____

OTHER_____

_____

_____

_____

_____

_____

_____

_____

_____

_____

_____

_____

_____

CHARACTER 4

FIRST_____MIDDLE_____LAST_____

NICKNAME_____

HAIR_COLOR_____STYLE_____

EYES_____GLASSES_____CONTACTS_____

SKIN_TONE_____TYPE_____

BUILD_____HEIGHT_____

D.O.B._____AGE_____

PLACE_OF_BIRTH_____

IDENTIFING_MARKS_____

CLOTHES_____

HEALTH_____

MOTHER_____

FATHER_____

SISTERS_____

BROTHERS_____

OTHER_FAMILY_____

HOME_LIFE_____

HOME_____LIVES_WITH_____

WORK_____DRIVES_____

SKILLS_____

SCHOOL_____

PETS_____

FRIENDS_____

GATHERING_PLACE_____

PHYSICAL_HABITS_____

VERBAL_HABITS_____

PEEVES_____

PERSONAL_ITEM_____

INTROVERT_____OR_EXTROVERT_____

TANGIBLE_THINGS_____OR_ABSTRACT_THINGS_____

TRUTH_&_LOGIC_____OR_ISSUES_&_CAUSES_____

STRUCTURED_____OR_UNSTRUCTURED_____

LIKES_____

DISLIKES_____

HOBBIES_____

TALENT_____

MEMMORY_OF_____

GOALS_____

FEARS_____

KNOWS_____

_____

DOESN'T_KNOW_____

_____

_____

OTHER_____

_____

_____

_____

_____

_____

_____

_____

_____

_____

_____

_____

_____

CHARACTER 5

FIRST_____MIDDLE_____LAST_____

NICKNAME_____

HAIR_COLOR_____STYLE_____

EYES_____GLASSES_____CONTACTS_____

SKIN_TONE_____TYPE_____

BUILD_____HEIGHT_____

D.O.B._____AGE_____

PLACE_OF_BIRTH_____

IDENTIFING_MARKS_____

CLOTHES_____

HEALTH_____

MOTHER_____

FATHER_____

SISTERS_____

BROTHERS_____

OTHER_FAMILY_____

HOME_LIFE_____

HOME_____LIVES_WITH_____

WORK_____DRIVES_____

SKILLS_____

SCHOOL_____

PETS_____

FRIENDS_____

GATHERING_PLACE_____

PHYSICAL_HABITS_____

VERBAL_HABITS_____

PEEVES_____

PERSONAL_ITEM_____

INTROVERT_____OR_EXTROVERT_____

TANGIBLE_THINGS_____OR_ABSTRACT_THINGS_____

TRUTH_&_LOGIC_____OR_ISSUES_&_CAUSES_____

STRUCTURED_____OR_UNSTRUCTURED_____

LIKES_____

DISLIKES_____

HOBBIES_____

TALENT_____

MEMMORY_OF_____

_____

GOALS_____

_____

FEARS_____

_____

KNOWS_____

_____

_____

DOESN'T_KNOW_____

_____

_____

_____

OTHER_____

_____

_____

_____

_____

_____

_____

_____

_____

_____

_____

_____

_____

_____

_____

CHARACTER 6

FIRST_____MIDDLE_____LAST_____

NICKNAME_____

HAIR_COLOR_____STYLE_____

EYES_____GLASSES_____CONTACTS_____

SKIN_TONE_____TYPE_____

BUILD_____HEIGHT_____

D.O.B._____AGE_____

PLACE_OF_BIRTH_____

IDENTIFING_MARKS_____

CLOTHES_____

HEALTH_____

MOTHER_____

FATHER_____

SISTERS_____

BROTHERS_____

OTHER_FAMILY_____

HOME_LIFE_____

HOME_____LIVES_WITH_____

WORK_____DRIVES_____

SKILLS_____

SCHOOL_____

PETS_____

FRIENDS_____

GATHERING_PLACE_____

PHYSICAL_HABITS_____

VERBAL_HABITS_____

PEEVES_____

PERSONAL_ITEM_____

INTROVERT_____OR_EXTROVERT_____

TANGIBLE_THINGS_____OR_ABSTRACT_THINGS_____

TRUTH_&_LOGIC_____OR_ISSUES_&_CAUSES_____

STRUCTURED_____OR_UNSTRUCTURED_____

LIKES_____

DISLIKES_____

HOBBIES_____

TALENT_____

MEMMORY_OF_____

_____

GOALS_____

_____

FEARS_____

_____

KNOWS_____

_____

_____

DOESN'T_KNOW_____

_____

_____

_____

OTHER_____

_____

_____

_____

_____

_____

_____

_____

_____

_____

_____

_____

_____

_____

_____

_____

CHARACTER 7

FIRST_____MIDDLE_____LAST_____

NICKNAME_____

HAIR_COLOR_____STYLE_____

EYES_____GLASSES_____CONTACTS_____

SKIN_TONE_____TYPE_____

BUILD_____HEIGHT_____

D.O.B._____AGE_____

PLACE_OF_BIRTH_____

IDENTIFING_MARKS_____

CLOTHES_____

HEALTH_____

MOTHER_____

FATHER_____

SISTERS_____

BROTHERS_____

OTHER_FAMILY_____

HOME_LIFE_____

HOME_____LIVES_WITH_____

WORK_____DRIVES_____

SKILLS_____

SCHOOL_____

PETS_____

FRIENDS_____

GATHERING_PLACE_____

PHYSICAL_HABITS_____

VERBAL_HABITS_____

PEEVES_____

PERSONAL_ITEM_____

INTROVERT_____OR_EXTROVERT_____

TANGIBLE_THINGS_____OR_ABSTRACT_THINGS_____

TRUTH_&_LOGIC_____OR_ISSUES_&_CAUSES_____

STRUCTURED_____OR_UNSTRUCTURED_____

LIKES_____

DISLIKES_____

HOBBIES_____

TALENT_____

MEMMORY_OF_____

_____

GOALS_____

_____

FEARS_____

_____

KNOWS_____

_____

_____

DOESN'T_KNOW_____

_____

_____

_____

OTHER_____

_____

_____

_____

_____

_____

_____

_____

_____

_____

_____

_____

_____

CHARACTER 8

FIRST_____MIDDLE_____LAST_____

NICKNAME_____

HAIR_COLOR_____STYLE_____

EYES_____GLASSES_____CONTACTS_____

SKIN_TONE_____TYPE_____

BUILD_____HEIGHT_____

D.O.B._____AGE_____

PLACE_OF_BIRTH_____

IDENTIFING_MARKS_____

CLOTHES_____

HEALTH_____

MOTHER_____

FATHER_____

SISTERS_____

BROTHERS_____

OTHER_FAMILY_____

HOME_LIFE_____

HOME_____LIVES_WITH_____

WORK_____DRIVES_____

SKILLS_____

SCHOOL_____

PETS_____

FRIENDS_____

GATHERING_PLACE_____

PHYSICAL_HABITS_____

VERBAL_HABITS_____

PEEVES_____

PERSONAL_ITEM_____

INTROVERT_____OR_EXTROVERT_____

TANGIBLE_THINGS_____OR_ABSTRACT_THINGS_____

TRUTH_&_LOGIC_____OR_ISSUES_&_CAUSES_____

STRUCTURED_____OR_UNSTRUCTURED_____

16

LIKES_____

DISLIKES_____

HOBBIES_____

TALENT_____

MEMMORY_OF_____

_____

GOALS_____

_____

FEARS_____

_____

KNOWS_____

_____

_____

DOESN'T_KNOW_____

_____

_____

_____

OTHER_____

_____

_____

_____

_____

_____

_____

_____

_____

_____

_____

_____

_____

_____

_____

CHARACTER 9

FIRST_____MIDDLE_____LAST_____

NICKNAME_____

HAIR_COLOR_____STYLE_____

EYES_____GLASSES_____CONTACTS_____

SKIN_TONE_____TYPE_____

BUILD_____HEIGHT_____

D.O.B._____AGE_____

PLACE_OF_BIRTH_____

IDENTIFING_MARKS_____

CLOTHES_____

HEALTH_____

MOTHER_____

FATHER_____

SISTERS_____

BROTHERS_____

OTHER_FAMILY_____

HOME_LIFE_____

HOME_____LIVES_WITH_____

WORK_____DRIVES_____

SKILLS_____

SCHOOL_____

PETS_____

FRIENDS_____

GATHERING_PLACE_____

PHYSICAL_HABITS_____

VERBAL_HABITS_____

PEEVES_____

PERSONAL_ITEM_____

INTROVERT_____OR_EXTROVERT_____

TANGIBLE_THINGS_____OR_ABSTRACT_THINGS_____

TRUTH_&_LOGIC_____OR_ISSUES_&_CAUSES_____

STRUCTURED_____OR_UNSTRUCTURED_____

18

LIKES_____

DISLIKES_____

HOBBIES_____

TALENT_____

MEMMORY_OF_____

_____

GOALS_____

_____

FEARS_____

_____

KNOWS_____

_____

_____

DOESN'T_KNOW_____

_____

_____

_____

OTHER_____

_____

_____

_____

_____

_____

_____

_____

_____

_____

_____

_____

_____

_____

CHARACTER 10

FIRST_____MIDDLE_____LAST_____

NICKNAME_____

HAIR_COLOR_____STYLE_____

EYES_____GLASSES_____CONTACTS_____

SKIN_TONE_____TYPE_____

BUILD_____HEIGHT_____

D.O.B._____AGE_____

PLACE_OF_BIRTH_____

IDENTIFING_MARKS_____

CLOTHES_____

HEALTH_____

MOTHER_____

FATHER_____

SISTERS_____

BROTHERS_____

OTHER_FAMILY_____

HOME_LIFE_____

HOME_____LIVES_WITH_____

WORK_____DRIVES_____

SKILLS_____

SCHOOL_____

PETS_____

FRIENDS_____

GATHERING_PLACE_____

PHYSICAL_HABITS_____

VERBAL_HABITS_____

PEEVES_____

PERSONAL_ITEM_____

INTROVERT_____OR_EXTROVERT_____

TANGIBLE_THINGS_____OR_ABSTRACT_THINGS_____

TRUTH_&_LOGIC_____OR_ISSUES_&_CAUSES_____

STRUCTURED_____OR_UNSTRUCTURED_____

20

LIKES_____

DISLIKES_____

HOBBIES_____

TALENT_____

MEMMORY_OF_____

_____

GOALS_____

_____

FEARS_____

_____

KNOWS_____

_____

_____

DOESN'T_KNOW_____

_____

_____

_____

OTHER_____

_____

_____

_____

_____

_____

_____

_____

_____

_____

_____

_____

_____

_____

CHARACTER 11

FIRST_____MIDDLE_____LAST_____

NICKNAME_____

HAIR_COLOR_____STYLE_____

EYES_____GLASSES_____CONTACTS_____

SKIN_TONE_____TYPE_____

BUILD_____HEIGHT_____

D.O.B._____AGE_____

PLACE_OF_BIRTH_____

IDENTIFING_MARKS_____

CLOTHES_____

HEALTH_____

MOTHER_____

FATHER_____

SISTERS_____

BROTHERS_____

OTHER_FAMILY_____

HOME_LIFE_____

HOME_____LIVES_WITH_____

WORK_____DRIVES_____

SKILLS_____

SCHOOL_____

PETS_____

FRIENDS_____

GATHERING_PLACE_____

PHYSICAL_HABITS_____

VERBAL_HABITS_____

PEEVES_____

PERSONAL_ITEM_____

INTROVERT_____OR_EXTROVERT_____

TANGIBLE_THINGS_____OR_ABSTRACT_THINGS_____

TRUTH_&_LOGIC_____OR_ISSUES_&_CAUSES_____

STRUCTURED_____OR_UNSTRUCTURED_____

LIKES_____

DISLIKES_____

HOBBIES_____

TALENT_____

MEMMORY_OF_____

_____

GOALS_____

_____

FEARS_____

_____

KNOWS_____

_____

_____

DOESN'T_KNOW_____

_____

_____

_____

OTHER_____

_____

_____

_____

_____

_____

_____

_____

_____

_____

_____

_____

_____

CHARACTER 12

FIRST_____MIDDLE_____LAST_____

NICKNAME_____

HAIR_COLOR_____STYLE_____

EYES_____GLASSES_____CONTACTS_____

SKIN_TONE_____TYPE_____

BUILD_____HEIGHT_____

D.O.B._____AGE_____

PLACE_OF_BIRTH_____

IDENTIFING_MARKS_____

CLOTHES_____

HEALTH_____

MOTHER_____

FATHER_____

SISTERS_____

BROTHERS_____

OTHER_FAMILY_____

HOME_LIFE_____

HOME_____LIVES_WITH_____

WORK_____DRIVES_____

SKILLS_____

SCHOOL_____

PETS_____

FRIENDS_____

GATHERING_PLACE_____

PHYSICAL_HABITS_____

VERBAL_HABITS_____

PEEVES_____

PERSONAL_ITEM_____

INTROVERT_____OR_EXTROVERT_____

TANGIBLE_THINGS_____OR_ABSTRACT_THINGS_____

TRUTH_&_LOGIC_____OR_ISSUES_&_CAUSES_____

STRUCTURED_____OR_UNSTRUCTURED_____

LIKES_____

DISLIKES_____

HOBBIES_____

TALENT_____

MEMMORY_OF_____

_____

GOALS_____

_____

FEARS_____

_____

KNOWS_____

_____

_____

DOESN'T_KNOW_____

_____

_____

_____

OTHER_____

_____

_____

_____

_____

_____

_____

_____

_____

_____

_____

_____

_____

_____

_____

CHARACTER 13

FIRST_____MIDDLE_____LAST_____

NICKNAME_____

HAIR_COLOR_____STYLE_____

EYES_____GLASSES_____CONTACTS_____

SKIN_TONE_____TYPE_____

BUILD_____HEIGHT_____

D.O.B._____AGE_____

PLACE_OF_BIRTH_____

IDENTIFING_MARKS_____

CLOTHES_____

HEALTH_____

MOTHER_____

FATHER_____

SISTERS_____

BROTHERS_____

OTHER_FAMILY_____

HOME_LIFE_____

HOME_____LIVES_WITH_____

WORK_____DRIVES_____

SKILLS_____

SCHOOL_____

PETS_____

FRIENDS_____

GATHERING_PLACE_____

PHYSICAL_HABITS_____

VERBAL_HABITS_____

PEEVES_____

PERSONAL_ITEM_____

INTROVERT_____OR_EXTROVERT_____

TANGIBLE_THINGS_____OR_ABSTRACT_THINGS_____

TRUTH_&_LOGIC_____OR_ISSUES_&_CAUSES_____

STRUCTURED_____OR_UNSTRUCTURED_____

LIKES_____

DISLIKES_____

HOBBIES_____

TALENT_____

MEMMORY_OF_____

_____

GOALS_____

_____

FEARS_____

_____

KNOWS_____

_____

_____

DOESN'T_KNOW_____

_____

_____

_____

OTHER_____

_____

_____

_____

_____

_____

_____

_____

_____

_____

_____

_____

_____

_____

CHARACTER 14

FIRST_____MIDDLE_____LAST_____

NICKNAME_____

HAIR_COLOR_____STYLE_____

EYES_____GLASSES_____CONTACTS_____

SKIN_TONE_____TYPE_____

BUILD_____HEIGHT_____

D.O.B._____AGE_____

PLACE_OF_BIRTH_____

IDENTIFING_MARKS_____

CLOTHES_____

HEALTH_____

MOTHER_____

FATHER_____

SISTERS_____

BROTHERS_____

OTHER_FAMILY_____

HOME_LIFE_____

HOME_____LIVES_WITH_____

WORK_____DRIVES_____

SKILLS_____

SCHOOL_____

PETS_____

FRIENDS_____

GATHERING_PLACE_____

PHYSICAL_HABITS_____

VERBAL_HABITS_____

PEEVES_____

PERSONAL_ITEM_____

INTROVERT_____OR_EXTROVERT_____

TANGIBLE_THINGS_____OR_ABSTRACT_THINGS_____

TRUTH_&_LOGIC_____OR_ISSUES_&_CAUSES_____

STRUCTURED_____OR_UNSTRUCTURED_____

LIKES_____

DISLIKES_____

HOBBIES_____

TALENT_____

MEMMORY_OF_____

_____

GOALS_____

_____

FEARS_____

_____

KNOWS_____

_____

_____

DOESN'T_KNOW_____

_____

_____

_____

OTHER_____

_____

_____

_____

_____

_____

_____

_____

_____

_____

_____

_____

_____

_____

29

CHARACTER 15

FIRST_____MIDDLE_____LAST_____

NICKNAME_____

HAIR_COLOR_____STYLE_____

EYES_____GLASSES_____CONTACTS_____

SKIN_TONE_____TYPE_____

BUILD_____HEIGHT_____

D.O.B._____AGE_____

PLACE_OF_BIRTH_____

IDENTIFING_MARKS_____

CLOTHES_____

HEALTH_____

MOTHER_____

FATHER_____

SISTERS_____

BROTHERS_____

OTHER_FAMILY_____

HOME_LIFE_____

HOME_____LIVES_WITH_____

WORK_____DRIVES_____

SKILLS_____

SCHOOL_____

PETS_____

FRIENDS_____

GATHERING_PLACE_____

PHYSICAL_HABITS_____

VERBAL_HABITS_____

PEEVES_____

PERSONAL_ITEM_____

INTROVERT_____OR_EXTROVERT_____

TANGIBLE_THINGS_____OR_ABSTRACT_THINGS_____

TRUTH_&_LOGIC_____OR_ISSUES_&_CAUSES_____

STRUCTURED_____OR_UNSTRUCTURED_____

LIKES_____

DISLIKES_____

HOBBIES_____

TALENT_____

MEMMORY_OF_____

_____

GOALS_____

_____

FEARS_____

_____

KNOWS_____

_____

_____

DOESN'T_KNOW_____

_____

_____

_____

OTHER_____

_____

_____

_____

_____

_____

_____

_____

_____

_____

_____

_____

_____

_____

_____

CHARACTER 16

FIRST_____MIDDLE_____LAST_____

NICKNAME_____

HAIR_COLOR_____STYLE_____

EYES_____GLASSES_____CONTACTS_____

SKIN_TONE_____TYPE_____

BUILD_____HEIGHT_____

D.O.B._____AGE_____

PLACE_OF_BIRTH_____

IDENTIFING_MARKS_____

CLOTHES_____

HEALTH_____

MOTHER_____

FATHER_____

SISTERS_____

BROTHERS_____

OTHER_FAMILY_____

HOME_LIFE_____

HOME_____LIVES_WITH_____

WORK_____DRIVES_____

SKILLS_____

SCHOOL_____

PETS_____

FRIENDS_____

GATHERING_PLACE_____

PHYSICAL_HABITS_____

VERBAL_HABITS_____

PEEVES_____

PERSONAL_ITEM_____

INTROVERT_____OR_EXTROVERT_____

TANGIBLE_THINGS_____OR_ABSTRACT_THINGS_____

TRUTH_&_LOGIC_____OR_ISSUES_&_CAUSES_____

STRUCTURED_____OR_UNSTRUCTURED_____

32

LIKES_____

DISLIKES_____

HOBBIES_____

TALENT_____

MEMMORY_OF_____

_____

GOALS_____

_____

FEARS_____

_____

KNOWS_____

_____

_____

DOESN'T_KNOW_____

_____

_____

_____

OTHER_____

_____

_____

_____

_____

_____

_____

_____

_____

_____

_____

_____

_____

_____

CHARACTER 17

FIRST_____MIDDLE_____LAST_____

NICKNAME_____

HAIR_COLOR_____STYLE_____

EYES_____GLASSES_____CONTACTS_____

SKIN_TONE_____TYPE_____

BUILD_____HEIGHT_____

D.O.B._____AGE_____

PLACE_OF_BIRTH_____

IDENTIFING_MARKS_____

CLOTHES_____

HEALTH_____

MOTHER_____

FATHER_____

SISTERS_____

BROTHERS_____

OTHER_FAMILY_____

HOME_LIFE_____

HOME_____LIVES_WITH_____

WORK_____DRIVES_____

SKILLS_____

SCHOOL_____

PETS_____

FRIENDS_____

GATHERING_PLACE_____

PHYSICAL_HABITS_____

VERBAL_HABITS_____

PEEVES_____

PERSONAL_ITEM_____

INTROVERT_____OR_EXTROVERT_____

TANGIBLE_THINGS_____OR_ABSTRACT_THINGS_____

TRUTH_&_LOGIC_____OR_ISSUES_&_CAUSES_____

STRUCTURED_____OR_UNSTRUCTURED_____

LIKES_____

DISLIKES_____

HOBBIES_____

TALENT_____

MEMMORY_OF_____

_____

GOALS_____

_____

FEARS_____

_____

KNOWS_____

_____

_____

DOESN'T_KNOW_____

_____

_____

_____

OTHER_____

_____

_____

_____

_____

_____

_____

_____

_____

_____

_____

_____

_____

CHARACTER 18

FIRST_____MIDDLE_____LAST_____

NICKNAME_____

HAIR_COLOR_____STYLE_____

EYES_____GLASSES_____CONTACTS_____

SKIN_TONE_____TYPE_____

BUILD_____HEIGHT_____

D.O.B._____AGE_____

PLACE_OF_BIRTH_____

IDENTIFING_MARKS_____

CLOTHES_____

HEALTH_____

MOTHER_____

FATHER_____

SISTERS_____

BROTHERS_____

OTHER_FAMILY_____

HOME_LIFE_____

HOME_____LIVES_WITH_____

WORK_____DRIVES_____

SKILLS_____

SCHOOL_____

PETS_____

FRIENDS_____

GATHERING_PLACE_____

PHYSICAL_HABITS_____

VERBAL_HABITS_____

PEEVES_____

PERSONAL_ITEM_____

INTROVERT_____OR_EXTROVERT_____

TANGIBLE_THINGS_____OR_ABSTRACT_THINGS_____

TRUTH_&_LOGIC_____OR_ISSUES_&_CAUSES_____

STRUCTURED_____OR_UNSTRUCTURED_____

LIKES_____

DISLIKES_____

HOBBIES_____

TALENT_____

MEMMORY_OF_____

_____

GOALS_____

_____

FEARS_____

_____

KNOWS_____

_____

_____

DOESN'T_KNOW_____

_____

_____

_____

OTHER_____

_____

_____

_____

_____

_____

_____

_____

_____

_____

_____

_____

_____

_____

CHARACTER 19

FIRST_____MIDDLE_____LAST_____

NICKNAME_____

HAIR_COLOR_____STYLE_____

EYES_____GLASSES_____CONTACTS_____

SKIN_TONE_____TYPE_____

BUILD_____HEIGHT_____

D.O.B._____AGE_____

PLACE_OF_BIRTH_____

IDENTIFING_MARKS_____

CLOTHES_____

HEALTH_____

MOTHER_____

FATHER_____

SISTERS_____

BROTHERS_____

OTHER_FAMILY_____

HOME_LIFE_____

HOME_____LIVES_WITH_____

WORK_____DRIVES_____

SKILLS_____

SCHOOL_____

PETS_____

FRIENDS_____

GATHERING_PLACE_____

PHYSICAL_HABITS_____

VERBAL_HABITS_____

PEEVES_____

PERSONAL_ITEM_____

INTROVERT_____OR_EXTROVERT_____

TANGIBLE_THINGS_____OR_ABSTRACT_THINGS_____

TRUTH_&_LOGIC_____OR_ISSUES_&_CAUSES_____

STRUCTURED_____OR_UNSTRUCTURED_____

LIKES_____

DISLIKES_____

HOBBIES_____

TALENT_____

MEMMORY_OF_____

_____

GOALS_____

_____

FEARS_____

_____

KNOWS_____

_____

_____

DOESN'T_KNOW_____

_____

_____

_____

OTHER_____

_____

_____

_____

_____

_____

_____

_____

_____

_____

_____

_____

_____

_____

_____

CHAPTER 20

FIRST_____MIDDLE_____LAST_____

NICKNAME_____

HAIR_COLOR_____STYLE_____

EYES_____GLASSES_____CONTACTS_____

SKIN_TONE_____TYPE_____

BUILD_____HEIGHT_____

D.O.B._____AGE_____

PLACE_OF_BIRTH_____

IDENTIFING_MARKS_____

CLOTHES_____

HEALTH_____

MOTHER_____

FATHER_____

SISTERS_____

BROTHERS_____

OTHER_FAMILY_____

HOME_LIFE_____

HOME_____LIVES_WITH_____

WORK_____DRIVES_____

SKILLS_____

SCHOOL_____

PETS_____

FRIENDS_____

GATHERING_PLACE_____

PHYSICAL_HABITS_____

VERBAL_HABITS_____

PEEVES_____

PERSONAL_ITEM_____

INTROVERT_____OR_EXTROVERT_____

TANGIBLE_THINGS_____OR_ABSTRACT_THINGS_____

TRUTH_&_LOGIC_____OR_ISSUES_&_CAUSES_____

STRUCTURED_____OR_UNSTRUCTURED_____

LIKES_____

DISLIKES_____

HOBBIES_____

TALENT_____

MEMMORY_OF_____

_____

GOALS_____

_____

FEARS_____

_____

KNOWS_____

_____

_____

DOESN'T_KNOW_____

_____

_____

_____

OTHER_____

_____

_____

_____

_____

_____

_____

_____

_____

_____

_____

_____

_____

41

14 PLACES

Places can be a home, friend's home, work place, coffee shop, town, street, trail, mountain or a friend's house. Anywhere that your characters go to include foreshadows plot turns and conjure mystery.

PLACE 1

ADDRESS_____

_____

_____   PHOTO

_____

_____

_____

_____

NOTES_____

_____

_____

_____

_____

_____

_____

_____

_____

_____

_____

_____

_____

_____

_____

_____

_____

PLACE 2

ADDRESS_____

_____

_____

PHOTO

_____

_____

_____

_____

NOTES_____

_____

_____

_____

_____

_____

_____

_____

_____

_____

_____

_____

_____

_____

_____

_____

_____

_____

PLACE 3

ADDRESS_____

_____

_____   PHOTO

_____

_____

_____

_____

NOTES_____

_____

_____

_____

_____

_____

_____

_____

_____

_____

_____

_____

_____

_____

_____

_____

_____

_____

_____

PLACE 4

ADDRESS_____

_____

_____   PHOTO

_____

_____

_____

_____

NOTES_____

_____

_____

_____

_____

_____

_____

_____

_____

_____

_____

_____

_____

_____

_____

_____

_____

PLACE 5

ADDRESS_____

_____

_____   PHOTO

_____

_____

_____

_____

NOTES_____

_____

_____

_____

_____

_____

_____

_____

_____

_____

_____

_____

_____

_____

_____

_____

_____

PLACE 6

ADDRESS_____

_____

PHOTO

_____

_____

_____

_____

_____

NOTES_____

_____

_____

_____

_____

_____

_____

_____

_____

_____

_____

_____

_____

_____

_____

_____

_____

_____

PLACE 7

ADDRESS_____

_____

_____   PHOTO

_____

_____

_____

_____

NOTES_____

_____

_____

_____

_____

_____

_____

_____

_____

_____

_____

_____

_____

_____

_____

_____

_____

_____

_____

_____

PLACE 8

ADDRESS_____

_____

_____   PHOTO

_____

_____

_____

_____

_____

NOTES_____

_____

_____

_____

_____

_____

_____

_____

_____

_____

_____

_____

_____

_____

_____

_____

_____

PLACE 9

ADDRESS_____

_____

_____   PHOTO

_____

_____

_____

_____

NOTES_____

_____

_____

_____

_____

_____

_____

_____

_____

_____

_____

_____

_____

_____

_____

_____

PLACE 10

ADDRESS_____

_____

_____   PHOTO

_____

_____

_____

_____

NOTES_____

_____

_____

_____

_____

_____

_____

_____

_____

_____

_____

_____

_____

_____

_____

_____

_____

PLACE 11

ADDRESS_____

_____

_____   PHOTO

_____

_____

_____

_____

NOTES_____

_____

_____

_____

_____

_____

_____

_____

_____

_____

_____

_____

_____

_____

_____

_____

_____

PLACE 12

ADDRESS_____

_____

_____

_____

_____

_____

_____

PHOTO

NOTES_____

_____

_____

_____

_____

_____

_____

_____

_____

_____

_____

_____

_____

_____

_____

_____

_____

PLACE 13

ADDRESS_____

_____

_____   PHOTO

_____

_____

_____

_____

NOTES_____

_____
_____
_____
_____
_____
_____
_____
_____
_____
_____
_____
_____
_____
_____
_____
_____
_____

PLACE 14

ADDRESS_____

_____

_____   PHOTO

_____

_____

_____

_____

_____

NOTES_____

_____

_____

_____

_____

_____

_____

_____

_____

_____

_____

_____

_____

_____

_____

_____

10 MAJOR EVENTS

Ten events that happen in just about every story and can become hard to track which character was involved or knows about each event.

1 INITIAL_EVENT:

DATE_____

WHERE_____

PEOPLE_INVOLVED_____

_____

_____

EVENT_____

_____

_____

ACTIONS_TAKEN_____

_____

_____

_____

_____

_____

_____

_____

_____

_____

_____

_____

_____

_____

PEOPLE_AFFECTED_____

_____

_____

_____

_____

_____

_____

_____

2 FIRST_POINT_OF_INTEREST:

DATE_____

WHERE_____

PEOPLE_INVOLVED_____

_____

_____

EVENT_____

_____

_____

ACTIONS_TAKEN_____

_____

_____

_____

_____

_____

_____

_____

_____

_____

_____

_____

_____

PEOPLE_AFFECTED_____

_____

_____

_____

_____

_____

_____

_____

3 SECCOND_EVENT:

DATE_____

WHERE_____

PEOPLE_INVOLVED_____

_____

_____

EVENT_____

_____

_____

ACTIONS_TAKEN_____

_____

_____

_____

_____

_____

_____

_____

_____

_____

_____

_____

_____

PEOPLE_AFFECTED_____

_____

_____

_____

_____

_____

_____

4 SECOND_POINT_OF_INTEREST:

DATE_____

WHERE_____

PEOPLE_INVOLVED_____

_____

_____

EVENT_____

_____

_____

ACTIONS_TAKEN_____

_____

_____

_____

_____

_____

_____

_____

_____

_____

_____

_____

_____

PEOPLE_AFFECTED_____

_____

_____

_____

_____

_____

_____

5 THIRD_EVENT:

DATE_____

WHERE_____

PEOPLE_INVOLVED_____

_____

_____

EVENT_____

_____

_____

ACTIONS_TAKEN_____

_____

_____

_____

_____

_____

_____

_____

_____

_____

_____

_____

_____

_____

PEOPLE_AFFECTED_____

_____

_____

_____

_____

_____

_____

_____

6 THIRD POINT OF INTEREST:

DATE_____

WHERE_____

PEOPLE_INVOLVED_____

_____

_____

EVENT_____

_____

_____

ACTIONS_TAKEN_____

_____

_____

_____

_____

_____

_____

_____

_____

_____

_____

_____

_____

_____

PEOPLE_AFFECTED_____

_____

_____

_____

_____

_____

_____

_____

7 FOURTH_EVENT:

DATE_____

WHERE_____

PEOPLE_INVOLVED_____

_____

_____

EVENT_____

_____

_____

ACTIONS_TAKEN_____

_____

_____

_____

_____

_____

_____

_____

_____

_____

_____

_____

_____

_____

PEOPLE_AFFECTED_____

_____

_____

_____

_____

_____

_____

_____

8 THE TRUTH BUILDS UP EVENT:

DATE_____

WHERE_____

PEOPLE_INVOLVED_____

_____

_____

EVENT_____

_____

_____

ACTIONS_TAKEN_____

_____

_____

_____

_____

_____

_____

_____

_____

_____

_____

_____

_____

PEOPLE_AFFECTED_____

_____

_____

_____

_____

_____

_____

_____

9 CLIMAXES_EVENT:

DATE_____

WHERE_____

PEOPLE_INVOLVED_____

_____

_____

EVENT_____

_____

_____

ACTIONS_TAKEN_____

_____

_____

_____

_____

_____

_____

_____

_____

_____

_____

_____

_____

PEOPLE_AFFECTED_____

_____

_____

_____

_____

_____

_____

10 SUMMAY_EVENT:

DATE_____

WHERE_____

PEOPLE_INVOLVED_____

_____

_____

EVENT_____

_____

_____

ACTIONS_TAKEN_____

_____

_____

_____

_____

_____

_____

_____

_____

_____

_____

_____

PEOPLE_AFFECTED_____

_____

_____

_____

_____

_____

_____

FIRST SENTENCE & PARAGRAPH

Extremely important information for the hook that lures your reader in to setting up your foreshadowing of the events about to unfold.

FIRST SENTENCE/PARAGRAPH

DISCUSSING THE CLIMAX

20 CHAPTERS INFO

It has been said that each chapter is worth reading if it has an event going on every four pages. So, the four-event set up is for a chapter with approximately sixteen to twenty pages in it. And with every action there is a reaction. Also to keep track of foreshadowing and their locations in the book they are also listed here. Finally the cliffhanger and the end of each chapter has your reader turning the pages and reading into the wee hours.

CHAPTER 1

FOUR EVENTS:

1_____

_____

_____

2_____

_____

_____

3_____

_____

_____

4_____

_____

_____

REACTIONS

_____

_____

_____

_____

_____

_____

_____

_____

_____

FORESHADOWS INVOLVED

_____

_____

_____

_____

_____

CHAPTER 2

FOUR EVENTS:

1_____

_____

_____

2_____

_____

_____

3_____

_____

_____

4_____

_____

_____

REACTIONS

_____

_____

_____

_____

_____

_____

_____

_____

FORESHADOWS

_____

_____

_____

_____

_____

CHAPTER 3

FOUR EVENTS:

1_____

_____

_____

2_____

_____

_____

3_____

_____

_____

4_____

_____

_____

REACTIONS

_____

_____

_____

_____

_____

_____

_____

_____

FORESHADOWS

_____

_____

_____

_____

CLIFFHANGER & OTHERS

CHAPTER 4

FOUR EVENTS:

1_____

_____

_____

2_____

_____

_____

3_____

_____

_____

4_____

_____

_____

REACTIONS

_____

_____

_____

_____

_____

_____

_____

_____

FORESHADOWS

_____

_____

_____

_____

_____

CHAPTER 5

FOUR EVENTS:

1_____

_____

_____

2_____

_____

_____

3_____

_____

_____

4_____

_____

_____

REACTIONS

_____

_____

_____

_____

_____

_____

_____

_____

_____

FORESHADOWS

_____

_____

_____

_____

_____

CLIFFHANGER & OTHERS

CHAPTER 6

FOUR EVENTS:

1_____

_____

_____

2_____

_____

_____

3_____

_____

_____

4_____

_____

_____

REACTIONS

_____

_____

_____

_____

_____

_____

_____

_____

_____

FORESHADOWS

_____

_____

_____

_____

_____

CHAPTER 7

FOUR EVENTS:

1_____

_____

_____

2_____

_____

_____

3_____

_____

_____

4_____

_____

_____

REACTIONS

_____

_____

_____

_____

_____

_____

_____

_____

_____

FORESHADOWS

_____

_____

_____

_____

_____

CLIFFHANGER & OTHERS

CHAPTER 8

FOUR EVENTS:

1_____

_____

_____

2_____

_____

_____

3_____

_____

_____

4_____

_____

_____

REACTIONS

_____

_____

_____

_____

_____

_____

_____

_____

FORESHADOWS

_____

_____

_____

_____

_____

CLIFFHANGER & OTHERS

CHAPTER 9

FOUR EVENTS:

1_____

_____

_____

2_____

_____

_____

3_____

_____

_____

4_____

_____

_____

REACTIONS

_____

_____

_____

_____

_____

_____

_____

_____

_____

FORESHADOWS

_____

_____

_____

_____

_____

CHAPTER 10

FOUR EVENTS:

1_____

_____

_____

2_____

_____

_____

3_____

_____

_____

4_____

_____

_____

REACTIONS

_____

_____

_____

_____

_____

_____

_____

_____

_____

FORESHADOWS

_____

_____

_____

_____

CHAPTER 11

FOUR EVENTS:

1_____

_____

_____

2_____

_____

_____

3_____

_____

_____

4_____

_____

_____

REACTIONS

_____

_____

_____

_____

_____

_____

_____

_____

_____

FORESHADOWS

_____

_____

_____

_____

_____

CLIFFHANGER & OTHERS

CHAPTER 12

FOUR EVENTS:

1_____

_____

_____

2_____

_____

_____

3_____

_____

_____

4_____

_____

_____

REACTIONS

_____

_____

_____

_____

_____

_____

_____

_____

FORESHADOWS

_____

_____

_____

_____

_____

CHAPTER 13

FOUR EVENTS:

1_____

_____

_____

2_____

_____

_____

3_____

_____

_____

4_____

_____

_____

REACTIONS

_____

_____

_____

_____

_____

_____

_____

_____

_____

FORESHADOWS

_____

_____

_____

_____

CLIFFHANGER & OTHERS

CHAPTER 14

FOUR EVENTS:

1_____

_____

_____

2_____

_____

_____

3_____

_____

_____

4_____

_____

_____

REACTIONS

_____

_____

_____

_____

_____

_____

_____

_____

_____

FORESHADOWS

_____

_____

_____

_____

_____

CHAPTER 15

FOUR EVENTS:

1_____

_____

_____

2_____

_____

_____

3_____

_____

_____

4_____

_____

_____

REACTIONS

_____

_____

_____

_____

_____

_____

_____

_____

FORESHADOWS

_____

_____

_____

_____

_____

CLIFFHANGER & OTHERS

CHAPTER 16

FOUR EVENTS:

1_____

_____

_____

2_____

_____

_____

3_____

_____

_____

4_____

_____

_____

REACTIONS

_____

_____

_____

_____

_____

_____

_____

_____

_____

FORESHADOWS

_____

_____

_____

_____

_____

CHAPTER 17

FOUR EVENTS:

1_____

_____

_____

2_____

_____

_____

3_____

_____

_____

4_____

_____

_____

REACTIONS

_____

_____

_____

_____

_____

_____

_____

_____

_____

FORESHADOWS

_____

_____

_____

_____

_____

CHAPTER 18

FOUR EVENTS:

1_____

_____

_____

2_____

_____

_____

3_____

_____

_____

4_____

_____

_____

REACTIONS

_____

_____

_____

_____

_____

_____

_____

_____

_____

FORESHADOWS

_____

_____

_____

_____

_____

CHAPTER 19

FOUR EVENTS:

1_____

_____

_____

2_____

_____

_____

3_____

_____

_____

4_____

_____

_____

REACTIONS

_____

_____

_____

_____

_____

_____

_____

_____

_____

FORESHADOWS

_____

_____

_____

_____

_____

CHAPTER 20

FOUR EVENTS:

1_____

_____

_____

2_____

_____

_____

3_____

_____

_____

4_____

_____

_____

REACTIONS

_____

_____

_____

_____

_____

_____

_____

_____

FORESHADOWS

_____

_____

_____

_____

LIST OF FORESHADOWS

All the details listed and sorted into each chapter and where each were solved. Leaving out the solution that were placed carefully for other books to follow in the series. Possibly underline these will show which have not been solved but should have compared to those of future tales. Appose to highlighting which can not be erased if you change your mind. The list of foreshadows plus the chapter it was mentioned in, and the chapter it was resolved in. If it was not resolved the future book in the series it will be resolved.

TIE IN ALMOST ALL FORESHADOWING

SHADOW	MENTIONED	RESOLVED
_____	_____	_____
_____	_____	_____
_____	_____	_____
_____	_____	_____
_____	_____	_____
_____	_____	_____
_____	_____	_____
_____	_____	_____
_____	_____	_____
_____	_____	_____
_____	_____	_____
_____	_____	_____
_____	_____	_____
_____	_____	_____
_____	_____	_____
_____	_____	_____
_____	_____	_____
_____	_____	_____
_____	_____	_____
_____	_____	_____
_____	_____	_____
_____	_____	_____
_____	_____	_____

SHADOW

_____
_____
_____
_____
_____
_____
_____
_____
_____
_____
_____
_____
_____
_____
_____
_____
_____
_____
_____
_____
_____
_____
_____
_____
_____
_____
_____
_____
_____
_____
_____

MENTIONED

_____
_____
_____
_____
_____
_____
_____
_____
_____
_____
_____
_____
_____
_____
_____
_____
_____
_____
_____
_____
_____
_____
_____
_____
_____
_____
_____
_____
_____
_____
_____

RESOLVED

_____
_____
_____
_____
_____
_____
_____
_____
_____
_____
_____
_____
_____
_____
_____
_____
_____
_____
_____
_____
_____
_____
_____
_____
_____
_____
_____
_____
_____
_____
_____

SHADOW	MENTIONED	RESOLVED
_____	_____	_____
_____	_____	_____
_____	_____	_____
_____	_____	_____
_____	_____	_____
_____	_____	_____
_____	_____	_____
_____	_____	_____
_____	_____	_____
_____	_____	_____
_____	_____	_____
_____	_____	_____
_____	_____	_____
_____	_____	_____
_____	_____	_____
_____	_____	_____
_____	_____	_____
_____	_____	_____
_____	_____	_____
_____	_____	_____
_____	_____	_____
_____	_____	_____
_____	_____	_____
_____	_____	_____
_____	_____	_____
_____	_____	_____

BUTTERFLY MOMENTS

The "wow" moments in each book that are said in a perfect quotable way. Sentences that can go in the description of the book or on the cover enticing you in to find out more. Or even better become the title of you story.

CALENDAR

Keep track of your character's meetings, appointments, starting a new job. When his or her enemy comes to town, whether they moved back or just "visiting." An important event your protagonist has eagerly waiting for, never again wonder, "Now when did that happen?"

JANUARY

SUNDAY	MONDAY	TUESDAY	WEDNESDAY	THURSDAY	FRIDAY	SATURDAY

FEBRUARY

SUNDAY	MONDAY	TUESDAY	WEDNESDAY	THURSDAY	FRIDAY	SATURDAY

MARCH

SUNDAY	MONDAY	TUESDAY	WEDNESDAY	THURSDAY	FRIDAY	SATURDAY

APRIL

SUNDAY	MONDAY	TUESDAY	WEDNESDAY	THURSDAY	FRIDAY	SATURDAY

MAY

SUNDAY	MONDAY	TUESDAY	WEDNESDAY	THURSDAY	FRIDAY	SATURDAY

JUNE

SUNDAY	MONDAY	TUESDAY	WEDNESDAY	THURSDAY	FRIDAY	SATURDAY

JULY

SUNDAY	MONDAY	TUESDAY	WEDNESDAY	THURSDAY	FRIDAY	SATURDAY

AUGUST

SUNDAY	MONDAY	TUESDAY	WEDNESDAY	THURSDAY	FRIDAY	SATURDAY

SEPTEMBER

SUNDAY	MONDAY	TUESDAY	WEDNESDAY	THURSDAY	FRIDAY	SATURDAY

OCTOBER

SUNDAY	MONDAY	TUESDAY	WEDNESDAY	THURSDAY	FRIDAY	SATURDAY

NOVEMBER

SUNDAY	MONDAY	TUESDAY	WEDNESDAY	THURSDAY	FRIDAY	SATURDAY

DECEMBER

SUNDAY	MONDAY	TUESDAY	WEDNESDAY	THURSDAY	FRIDAY	SATURDAY

6 FAMILY TREES

Who is related to who? Was she her Grandmother who past or Great Grandmother? Was the mentioned relative alive when an event happened in the past? No more guessing and making needless little mistakes in your next book in the series. Or later in the same book.

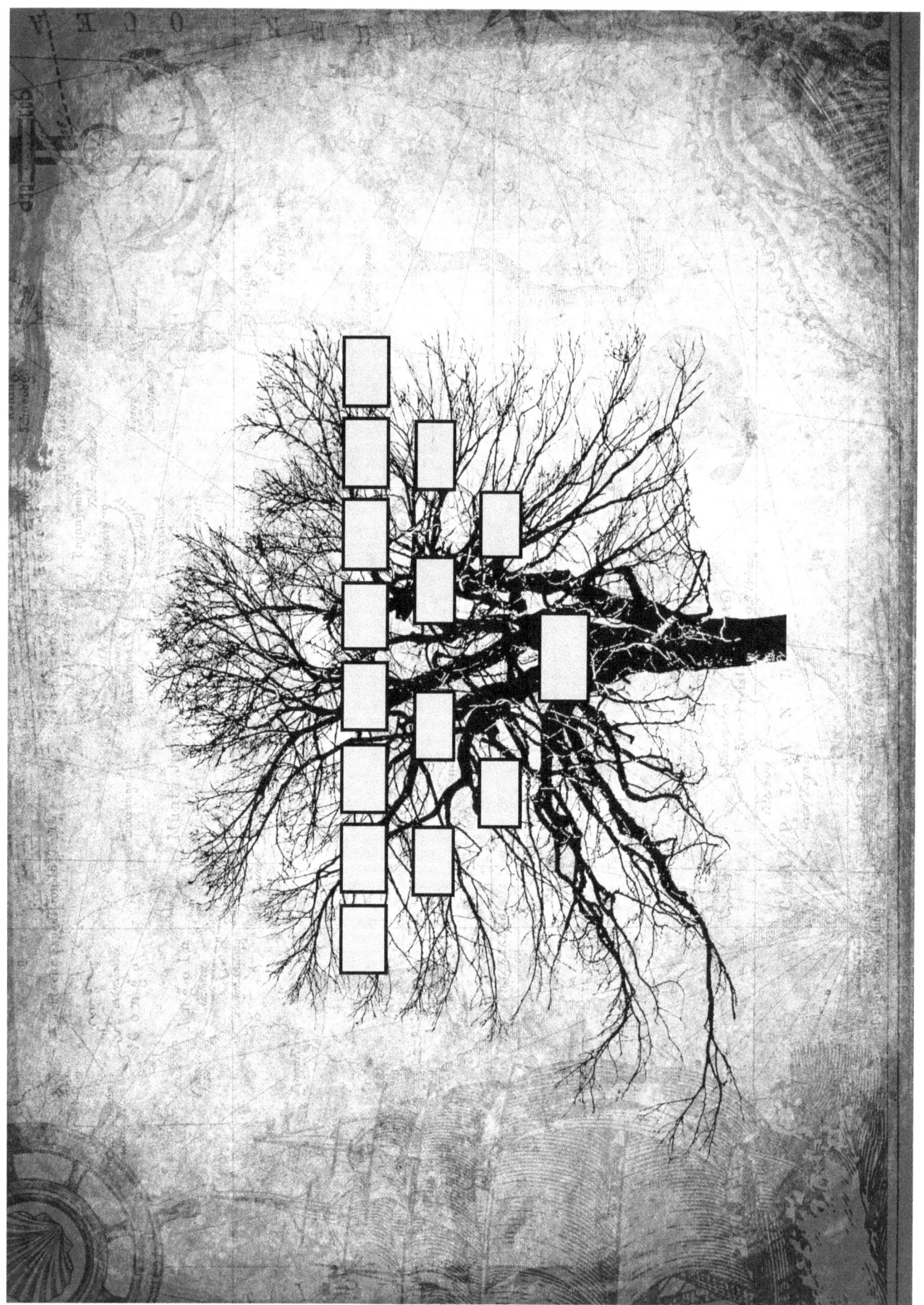

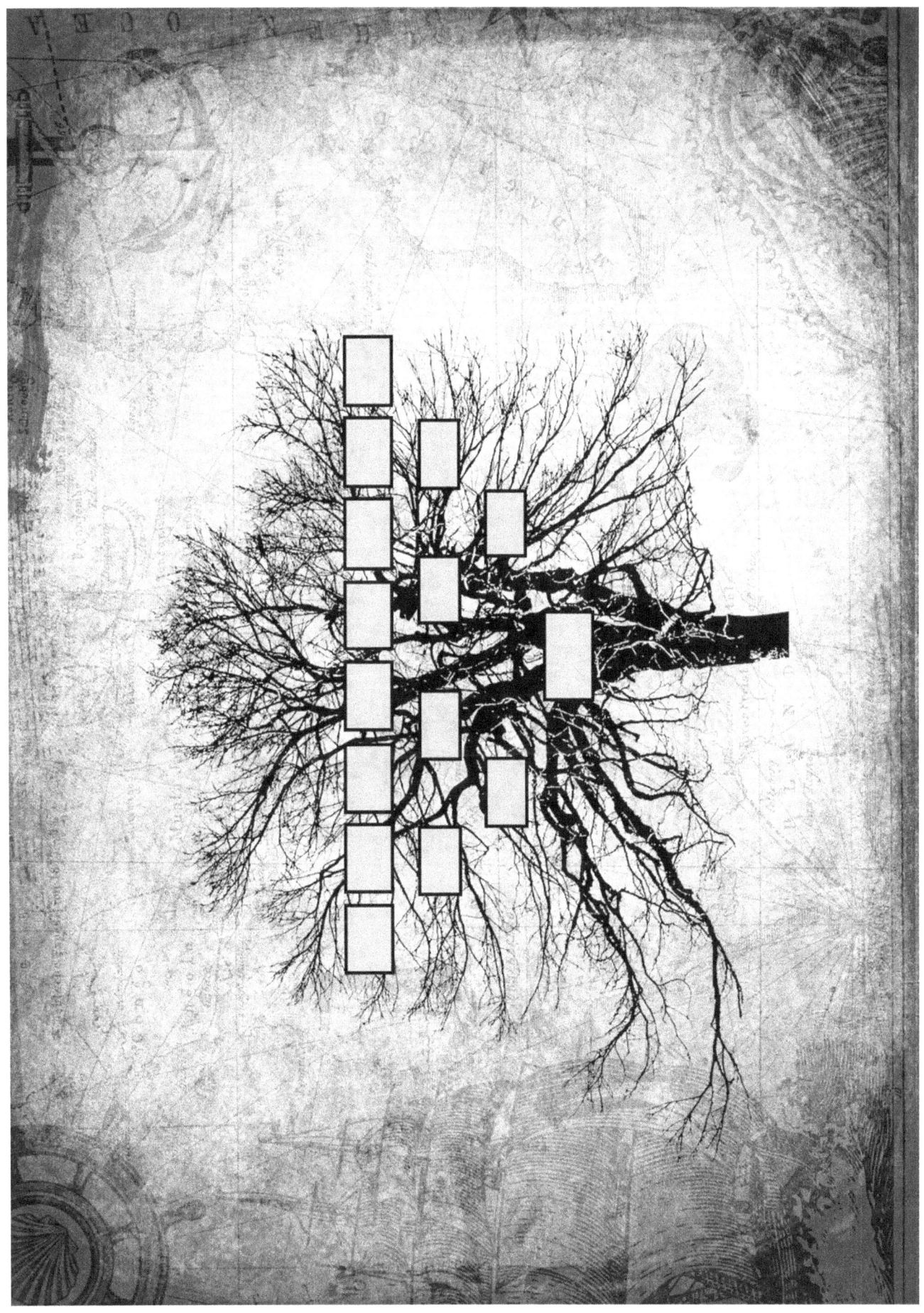

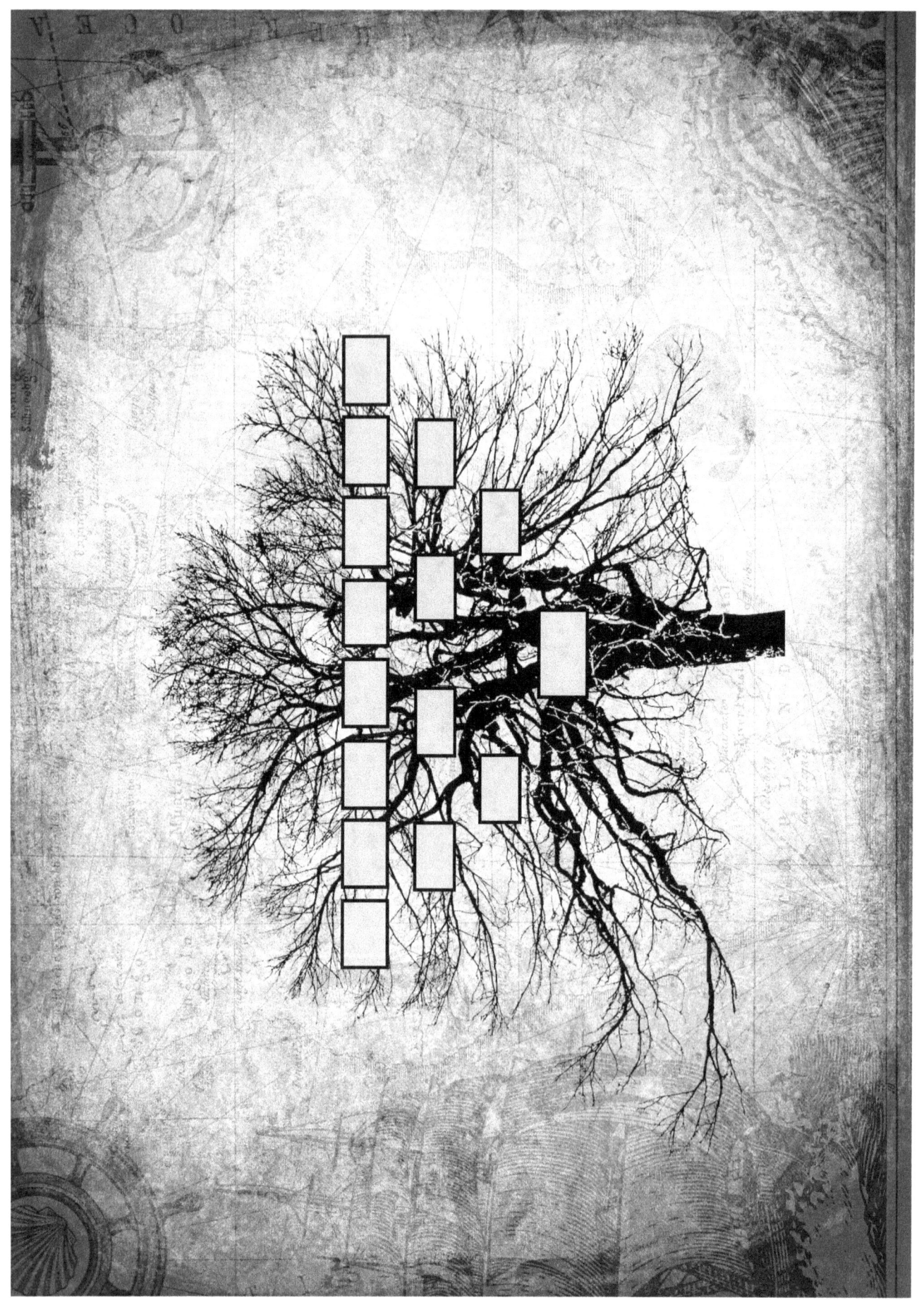

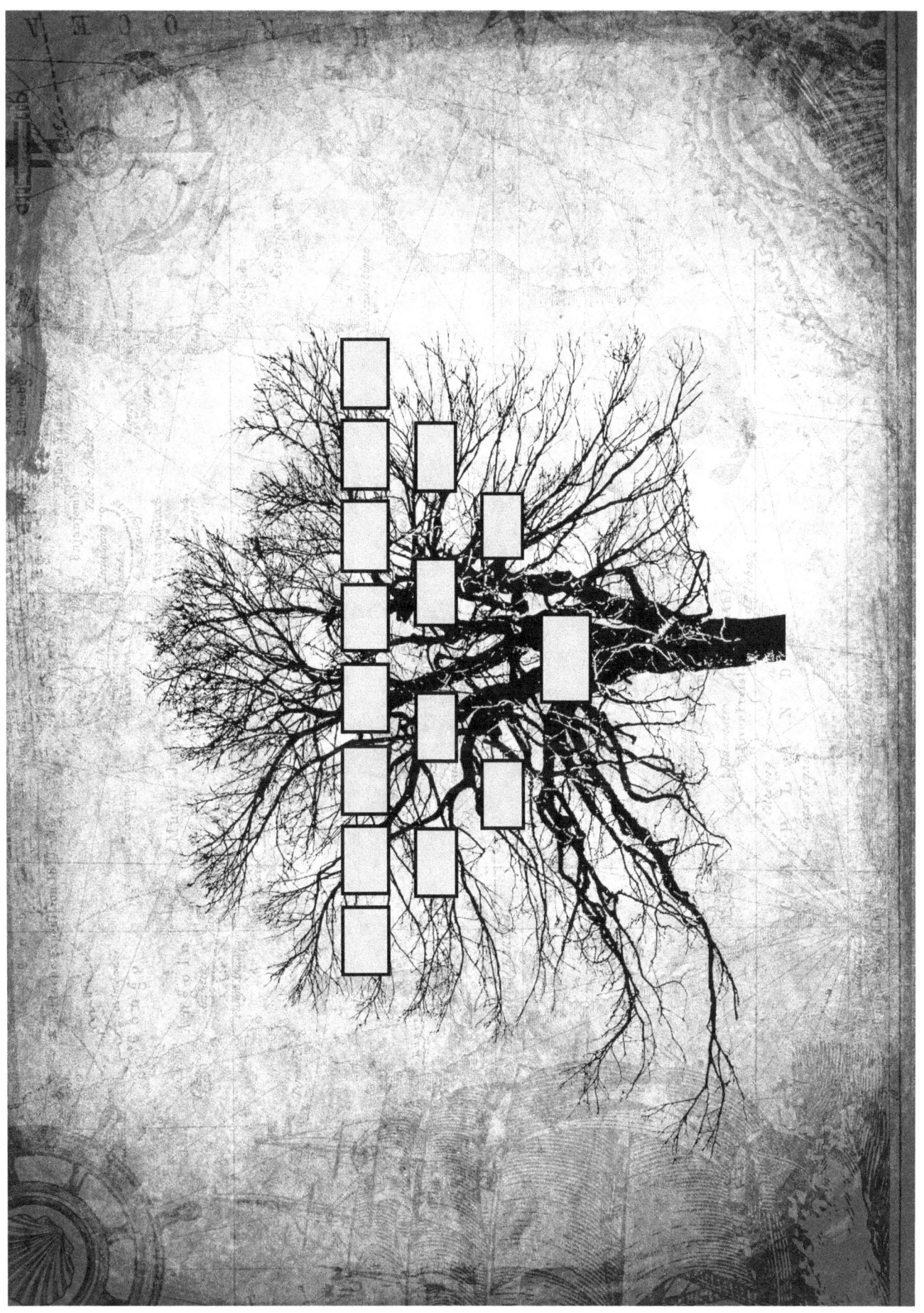

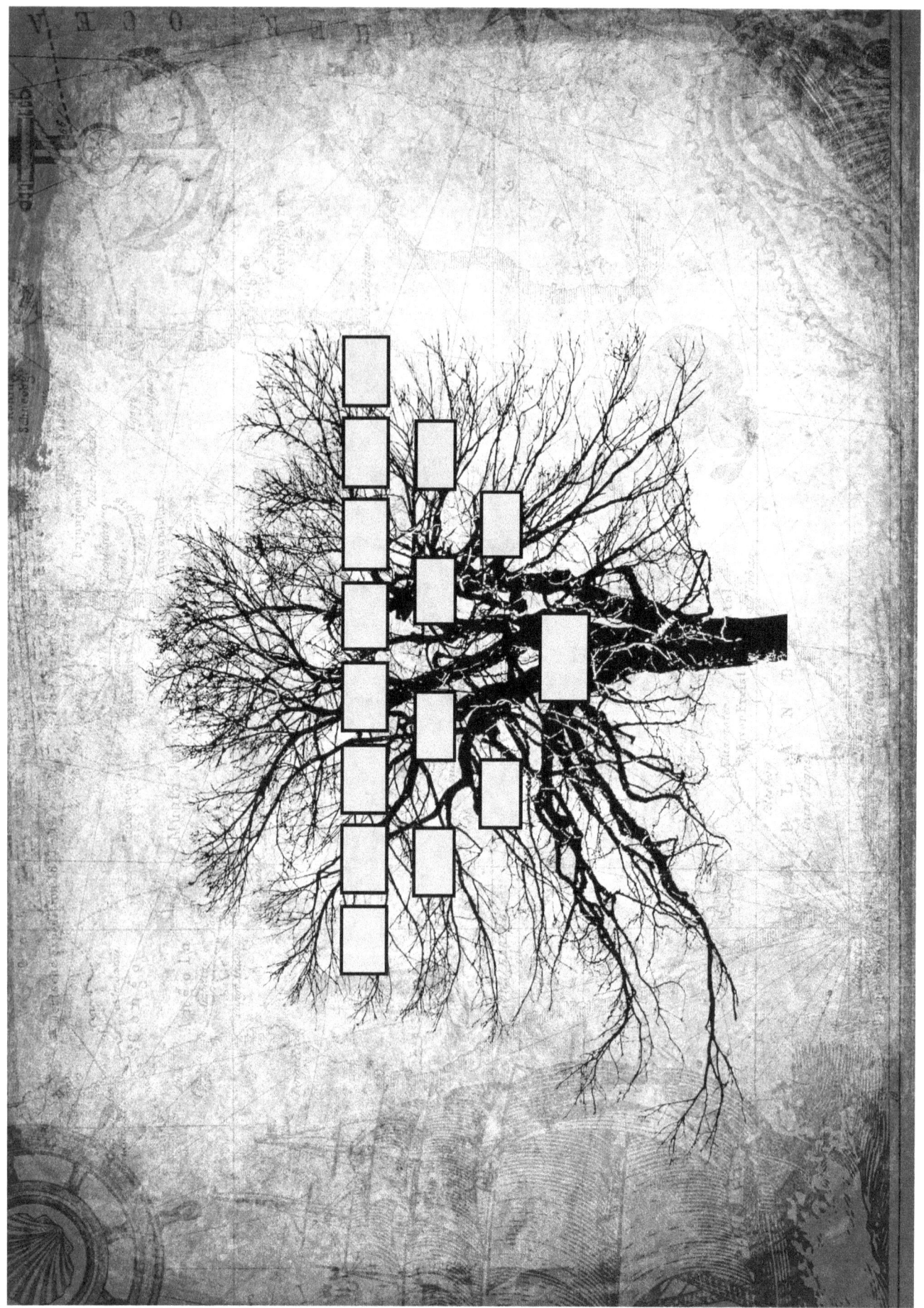

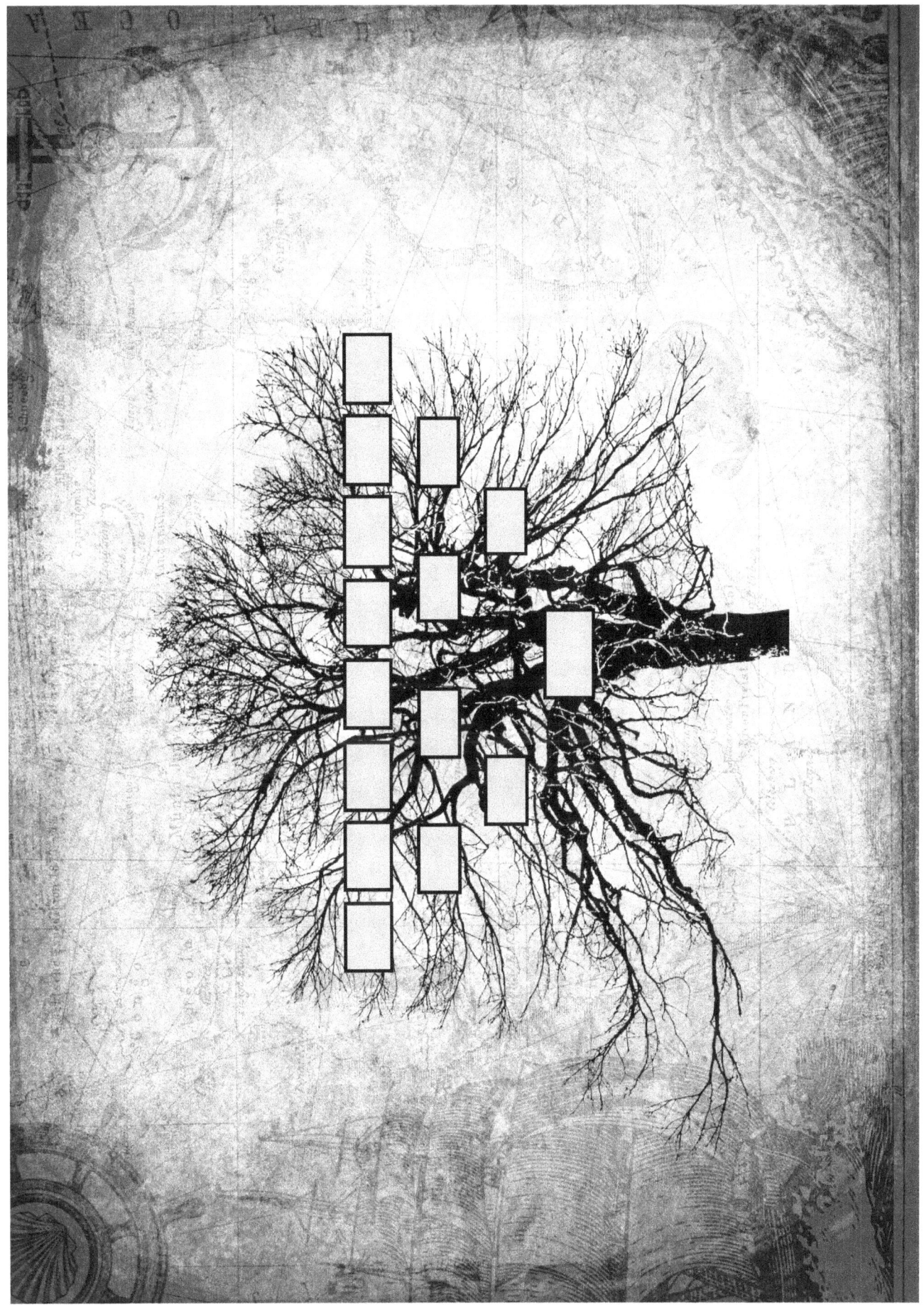

151

Author page

www.ingramcontent.com/pod-product-compliance
Lightning Source LLC
Chambersburg PA
CBHW081351280526
45788CB00009B/2843